MAKE & SHARE
RANDOM ACTS OF KINDNESS

MAKE & SHARE
RANDOM ACTS OF KINDNESS

Simple Crafts and Recipes to Give and Spread Joy

MIQUE PROVOST

Creator of THIRTY HANDMADE DAYS

Photography by Alyssa Bazar

PAGE STREET
PUBLISHING CO.

PAGE STREET
PUBLISHING CO.

Copyright © 2015 Mique Provost

First published in 2015 by
Page Street Publishing Co.
27 Congress Street, Suite 103
Salem, MA 01970
www.pagestreetpublishing.com

Distributed by Macmillan, sales in Canada by The Canadian Manda Group.

18   17   16   15   1   2   3   4   5

ISBN-13: 978-1-62414-192-8
ISBN-10: 1-62414-192-7

Library of Congress Control Number: 2015949397

Cover and book design by Page Street Publishing Co.
Photography by Alyssa Bazar

Printed and bound in the USA

Page Street is proud to be a member of 1% for the Planet. Members donate one percent of their sales to one or more of the over 1,500 environmental and sustainability charities across the globe who participate in this program.

DEDICATION

This book is dedicated to the people who surround me and make every day brighter: my husband, Josh, and my kids, Jonathan, Julia and Andrew. They make me laugh, make me proud, make me crazy and have taught me what true love is all about.

To my Mom and Dad who steered my "determinedness" in the right way and taught me to be kind and thoughtful. And to my sister, Jessica, and brother, Tony, who put up with me in childhood and who I am grateful to now count as friends.

I love you all.

CONTENTS

INTRODUCTION

A few years ago we were stumped for what to give my oldest child for his thirteenth birthday, just like in previous years. Jonathan was diagnosed with autism at two years old. He has the biggest heart and is the epitome of unconditional love, but he can be a challenge to buy gifts for. For his big teenage year, we had no suggestions for our family and friends who begged for an idea. And then it hit me. We were going to have a random-acts-of-kindness day in honor of him.

I was afraid to hit "send" on my status updates and emails, but did it anyway. Would anyone want to join in? Instead of buying presents that (although well-intentioned and appreciated) our JJ wouldn't get excited about, I wanted to spread some love around.

The day unfolded in a magical way. In a 24-hour period my heart grew two sizes. I had family who jumped at the chance to celebrate Jonathan. There were friends who joined in on the fun. I was floored to hear from people I had never met but who wanted to be a part of our day. There were hundreds of random acts of kindness performed and tears streamed down my face as I read each one. Not only had our random acts of kindness helped the strangers we served, the amount of joy that we experienced on the giving end was indescribable. I made it a goal to do random acts of kindness every month for the year. I learned a lot about stepping out of my comfort zone, looking for people in need and doing things without expectations, *just because*.

My intention with this book is to inspire you to make and share random acts of kindness. You don't have to do a whole day, and you don't have to do it every month; just take what works for you and go for it!

"Do your little bit of good right where you are;
it's those little bits put together that
overwhelm the world."
—Desmond Tutu

HOW TO USE THIS BOOK

This book was created to encourage kindness. Think of it as a jumping-off point. It is meant to inspire you to look for ways to improve your surroundings through random acts of kindness. The actions can take place within your community, within your relationships, within the walls of your home and more.

In this book, you will find simple recipes that are some of our family favorites, craft projects that can be completed on your own or with your family and tear-out designs to use for your random acts of kindness.

Each project is marked with a symbol (or two) to note what it is geared toward.

= within your community

= within your friend and family life

= with kids in mind

I want to inspire you to be open and aware of opportunities for kindness and service. Just by picking up this book, you are already ahead of the game!

You might not always have the time to do big, over-the-top random acts of kindness. But every day there's a chance to help, uplift or impact others in a positive way.

When I set out to do random acts of kindness every month, it became crystal clear that I had blinders on to other people's needs. Sure, I pitched in when people asked, but I was so focused on daily tasks that I didn't recognize opportunities for service. After spending some time searching for ways to help, my eyes were opened to a different way of thinking and living. The same thing can happen to you. So let's get started, shall we?

3 THINGS TO KEEP IN MIND BEFORE YOU GET STARTED

1. Make a conscious effort to be more aware.

Half of the battle is being aware. When you make the decision to give of yourself, paying attention to the world around you is key. When you look for opportunities to serve, you will find them everywhere.

2. Step out of your comfort zone.

I was surprised at how uncomfortable it felt at first to do nice things for unsuspecting people. What if they reject me? What if they think it's silly or dumb? What if, what if, what if!? It can feel awkward to walk up to someone randomly. But the more you do it, the less awkward you feel. If you do get rejected, it is on them, not on you. If you've made the effort and they aren't okay with it, at least you know that you tried to fill a need wanting nothing in return.

3. Practice makes progress.

Throw the old saying "practice makes perfect" right out the window. We're not looking for perfection here. Doing random acts of kindness is about looking outside of Y-O-U and making this world a happier place. Doing any small act is a step in the right direction. So just get out there and do it!

THE JACKET OFF HIS BACK

I was driving to work. It was really cold outside, about 14°F (-10°C). When I had almost gotten to my office, I came around a corner and saw a guy in a light jumpsuit huddled against a sign, looking cold. I drove past and pulled into the parking lot at my job half a block away. I sat in the parking lot for a few seconds with butterflies in my stomach because I knew what I was going to do, and it was a little outside my comfort zone. I pulled out and drove back over to the guy. I had taken my jacket off beforehand because I didn't want him to feel like he was taking the jacket off my back. I don't remember much about the conversation we had, but he took the jacket gratefully and put it on right away. I felt like a better person that day.

—Devin Pitcher

This story is especially personal as Devin was the first person to join in on my random-acts-of-kindness day for my son's birthday. He hadn't met my son Jonathan before, but wanted to get involved. It brought tears to my eyes that he was moved to literally give the jacket off his back for a stranger.

TRADITIONAL SMALL & SIMPLE ACTS THAT MAKE ALL THE DIFFERENCE

Not sure if you're ready for the big stuff? Tackle one or all of these traditional random-act-of-kindness ideas.

Usually the hardest part of doing something new and unfamiliar is taking that first conscious step. First, decide that you're going to do it. Then, take a deep breath and make the leap! Don't let your fear get the better of you. Once you've taken the leap and done your first act of kindness, it will be easier and easier every time.

1. Smile at every person you come in contact with for an hour.
2. Open the door for people wherever you go.
3. Give a compliment to someone in line at the store.
4. Pay for someone behind you in the drive-thru.
5. Give a nice tip to a server at a restaurant.
6. Deliver cans to a homeless shelter.
7. Put carts away in a parking lot.
8. Leave change in a vending machine.
9. Let someone go in front of you in line.
10. Give someone your parking spot.
11. Donate to charity at a checkout line when asked.
12. Put money in a meter that is about to expire.
13. Volunteer your time in a classroom.
14. Offer your seat on a plane, train or bus.
15. Bring in your neighbors' trash cans.
16. Help someone move.
17. Donate blood.
18. Call someone who you've lost touch with.
19. Leave extra coupons for items on a grocery store shelf.
20. Donate clothes to charity.
21. Pick up trash at a park.
22. Volunteer at a homeless shelter.
23. Support local charity organizations by purchasing items (Girl Scout cookies, magazine drives, etc.).
24. Shovel snow or rake leaves for a neighbor.
25. Donate supplies to your school.

LETTERS *for* TROOPS

I've had members of my family serve in the military. They left their home and family to defend our country. There are thousands of people all over the world who are missing those they love most.

This is a small gesture to remind them that you appreciate their service. This is a great act to do with your kids to encourage gratitude.

SUPPLIES NEEDED

Tear-out design (page 129)

Pen

Envelope

Stamp

INSTRUCTIONS

Use the "Dear Service Member" tear-out design to write a note and let members of the military know you are grateful and thinking of them.

You can take this idea one step further and send care packages to service members as well. Check online at http://letterstosoldiers.org/ or http://soldiersangels.org/letter-writing-team.html. You can also visit local organizations to see what type of needs deployed military members might have.

"Wherever there is a human in need, there is an opportunity for kindness and to make a difference."
-Kevin Heath

HANDMADE TOYS
for AN ANIMAL SHELTER

People in the community aren't the only ones who can benefit from kindness—don't forget your furry friends! These simple-to-make toys will help animals that need a little extra attention feel loved.

SUPPLIES NEEDED

Empty water bottle

Fleece fabric

Scissors

INSTRUCTIONS

Lay the empty water bottle on top of the fleece fabric. (Note: You do not want the heaviest fleece, but not the lightest either. Something in between would be ideal.)

Trim the fabric leaving approximately 3 inches (about 7.6 cm) of excess fabric on either side. Fold the fabric in half with the pretty side inside, and stitch a straight line allowing enough room for the water bottle to slide in snugly. If you don't have a sewing machine, you can easily hand-stitch the fabric together. Turn the fabric right side out. Slide the water bottle into the tube of fabric. Cut two strips of fabric to tie around either end of the water bottle.

At this point, you should have a tightly fit water bottle with two ends tied and some excess fabric hanging over on either side. Cut slits in the fabric to make pom-pom–looking ends. Animals will love being able to play with the strings on the end and the crinkly noise that the water bottle makes.

SIMPLE ACT ALTERNATIVE

Animal shelters are always in need of blankets, sheets and towels. Set aside gently used items to donate to your local shelter.

Heartfelt HEART ATTACK

Everybody needs a little pick-me-up out of the blue. Show your family members or friends how much you love and appreciate them with this heartwarming craft project. All it takes is a little time and some heartfelt messages to complete this project. A heart attack never felt so good!

SUPPLIES NEEDED

Tear-out design (page 131)
Construction paper
Scissors
Pen/marker
Craft sticks
Glue or glue dots

INSTRUCTIONS

Using the supplied template, trace heart shapes onto construction paper. Cut around the hearts.

Using the pen or marker, write uplifting messages on the hearts. It could be reasons why you love your friends or family members, their best qualities or sayings like, "You are the best!"

Adhere a craft stick to the back of each heart using glue or a glue dot.

Place the heart sticks in front of their home in the grass or deliver in a potted plant.

"We rise by lifting others."
—Robert Ingersoll

WE HOPE THIS BAG IS A
blessing
TO YOU ♥

BLESSING BAGS
for THE HOMELESS

If you are looking to help those in need with tangible items, this blessing bag project is a great place to start.

These bags are intended to help people without homes—either with a delivery to a homeless shelter or to have on hand in your car or carryall. I've listed a few good staples, but you can also include seasonal items and gifts or a handwritten note for an added touch. Contact your local homeless shelter to ask specific questions about what types of items their residents are in need of.

SUPPLIES NEEDED

Socks

Deodorant

Toothbrushes & tooth paste

Small packs of tissues

Nonperishable food

Water bottles

Small bottles of hand sanitizer

Bars of soap

Zip-close bags

Brown bags or gift bags

Tear-out design (page 133)

INSTRUCTIONS

Place one of each of the staple items into each zip-close bag. Place each zip-close bag inside a brown bag or a gift bag and attach a copy of the tear-out design on the outside.

CAR WASH *for* A NEIGHBOR

Feel like making someone's day just a little bit better? Why not wash their car and leave an inspiring note on their windshield? This idea is probably better suited for the warmer months of the year when it's comfortable to be outside.

SUPPLIES NEEDED

Bucket

Soap

Water

Towels

Tear-out design (page 135)

INSTRUCTIONS

Gather the car-washing supplies and get to work! Spend a few minutes making your neighbor's car shine brighter and let them know that someone is thinking of them. After you've dried it off with the towels, add the personalized tag to their windshield.

Colorful POM-POM BLOOMS

With this simple random act of kindness, you'll have the opportunity to brighten someone's day with bouquets of flowers that will last forever. Learn how to make pom-pom flowers and deliver them to a mental health treatment facility, a nursing home or any local residence for patients needing a little extra attention.

Call ahead to make sure that patients can receive gifts from visitors. When you arrive to deliver, you can drop them off at the front desk and allow them to pass them out to patients they think could use them. Or you can talk to them about delivering them yourself.

SUPPLIES NEEDED

Assorted colors of yarn

Scissors

Sticks, faux floral stems or pipe cleaners

Hot glue gun

Tear-out design (page 137)

INSTRUCTIONS

For each pom-pom flower, you will do the following (see photos):

Using the yarn, wrap it around three fingers close together 50 or more times. This will create a smaller pom-pom. You can wrap more for a bigger pom-pom. Cut the yarn off of the spool.

The second part of this is a little bit tricky, but it gets easier the more pom-poms you make. You'll cut one strand of yarn to approximately 10 inches (about 25 cm). Thread it through the middle of your fingers.

Then pull the other side of the yarn up and over. Flip your hand over and tie the two ends of the single strand together loosely.

Slide the wrapped yarn off and pull the single strand of yarn tight. Tie a knot at the end to secure it.

Slide your scissors into the loops of the pom-pom and cut them all on both sides. Fluff your pom-pom and hide the tie within the middle. Cut the excess strings on the pom-pom to make it even.

Now, your pom-pom is ready for the stems. To secure, use a dot of hot glue around the top of the stem and push it into the middle of the pom-pom.

Make several pom-poms for a bouquet. Tie them together with another piece of yarn or ribbon. Attach the supplied tag.

MUFFINS FOR FIREMEN & POLICE OFFICERS

I've always admired those who choose a career helping others. Firefighters and police officers do that every single day. They put their lives on the line to protect and help their community members.

Make a delicious treat, attach a thank-you note and show support and appreciation for all that they do.

It is a good idea to call your local fire station or police station before delivering these treats. You can find the best nonemergency phone number to call by searching online. They will let you know if they accept food items and when is the best time to drop them off.

CINI-MINI DONUT MUFFINS

These cini-mini muffins are the perfect size. They are sugary sweet and sure to put a smile on any service officer's face!

FOR THE MUFFINS

2 eggs
1 cup (240 ml) whole milk
⅔ cup (160 g) unsalted butter, melted
3 cups (360 g) all-purpose flour
1 cup (200 g) sugar
3 tsp (15 g) baking powder
¼ tsp salt

FOR THE TOPPING

1 cup (200 g) sugar
2 tsp (5 g) cinnamon
1 cup (240 g) unsalted butter, melted

INSTRUCTIONS

Preheat the oven to 350°F (175°C). Grease your mini muffin tin with cooking spray or butter and flour.

Combine the first three ingredients and set aside. Mix the dry ingredients together.

Gradually add the wet mix to the dry mix until combined.

Fill the muffin cups two-thirds of the way full. I like to use an ice cream or cookie scoop for even distribution.

Bake for 20 minutes or until golden brown. Let cool.

While cooling, combine the cinnamon and sugar in a small bowl. Dip the cooled muffins one at a time into the melted butter and then into the cinnamon-sugar mix until coated.

Package these muffins up and add a cute tag to say thank you!

You can use the thank-you tag on page 139.

"I would maintain that thanks are the highest form of thought; and that gratitude is happiness doubled by wonder."

—G.K. Chesterton

WE WILL NEVER FORGET

We lived in Washington, D.C., during 9/11 and experienced all the raw emotion that came with that period in our nation's history. When we moved to California we felt disconnected, and I wanted to do something on what is now Patriot's Day to aid in our healing and honor the memory of those who were lost. Each year we write letters and bake something sweet and special, then take them to our local fire department. Some years we even bring handmade blankets, which firefighters can give to those in need. I feel it is important for our family to keep a connection to 9/11, so we never forget.

—Amanda Niederhauser

TIPS *for* TEACHING KIDS TO BE KIND

Seeing children light up because they feel good from helping someone is the most wonderful experience. Doing random acts of kindness can help teach kids to think outside of themselves and give them the opportunity to have fun in the process. In addition to showing them how to create specific projects, teaching kids to be kind people is important.

WHY IS KINDNESS IMPORTANT?

Take the time to have conversations with your children on why kindness matters. Why is kindness important to you? What does being kind mean? Discuss how being kind or unkind can impact a situation.

RECOGNIZE KINDNESS.

The ultimate goal is to raise kind people who go and do good in the world. Not every act needs to be noted, but kids will be more apt to be kind and seek out ways to help if they are recognized for it.

KINDNESS BEGINS WITH YOU.

The old saying, "Do as I say, not as I do," does not apply. Kids definitely learn from the people who surround them most, especially their parents. If their parents are kind, they have a much higher likelihood of being kind as well. By making sure to use kind words and doing kind deeds, you are modeling for your child(ren) the way to be kind. Though other people who surround them can influence them, it's your job as a parent to teach your kids to be thoughtful, empathetic and kind.

IT'S NEVER TOO LATE.

Whether you have a six-month-old child or a 16-year-old, it's never too early or too late to teach kindness and service. Start now!

"I actually think that the most efficacious way of making a difference is to lead by example, and doing random acts of kindness is setting a very good example of how to behave in the world."
—Misha Collins

Family KINDNESS JAR

Set aside some time as a family to create a simple random acts of kindness jar. With this jar, you will not only make lasting memories but also do good in the community, too.

SUPPLIES NEEDED

Jar

Pens

Tear-out design (page 141)

Markers and crayons

Paper

INSTRUCTIONS

All different kinds of jars could be used for this activity. The idea is simply to instill kindness in your home. It will also encourage family members to look outside of themselves and to serve others.

For a family night, gather together and create a list of random acts of kindness that you want to do together. This could be once a month, once a week, to celebrate someone's birthday or whatever works best for your family situation. Use the tear-out design on page 141 as a guide for this activity.

Have each family member write down what they'd like to do (either individually or as a family) and add it to the kindness jar.

You can decorate the jar using markers, crayons and paper. Get creative!

"A kind and compassionate act is often its own reward."
—William John Bennett

BEARS *for* ORPHANAGES

Make these super simple stuffed bears to donate to orphanages around the world or to local kids' organizations. Kids can help making these adorable bears and enjoy knowing that their creations will be going to a good home.

Before starting this project, search for national organizations online who accept donations of this kind. There are many sites that include lists of charities looking for handmade toys. Handcrafting with Love is a great place to start: http://www.handcraftingwithlove.net/charity/hcharity.html.

SUPPLIES NEEDED

Hand towel

Black felt

Hot-glue gun or embroidery thread

Buttons

Batting for stuffing

INSTRUCTIONS

There are several ways to put together these bears. You can use a sewing machine or hand-stitch them—whatever you have on hand and are comfortable with! Use photos as a guide.

First, fold over the hand towel. Using your hand as a guide, cut out two body parts. Then, using the excess from the hand towel, cut out four semi circles for a set of two ears. Next, cut out a triangle shape from the black felt. This will be the bear's nose. Cut out black felt inner ear shapes and shape for mouth as shown in photos.

On the bear's face (the fuzzy towel side), you can either glue or sew buttons on for eyes. Then, either glue or sew on the felt nose, inner ears and mouth.

Next, you'll sandwich the bear ears in the middle of the body (which is right sides together to sew). You will have the bear top with the face on it, two ears facing downward with the ends sticking through the top of the bear and the underside of the bear facing together.

Sew around the outside of the body making sure to catch the ears in the sewing. Leave an opening on the bottom of the body.

Turn the bear right sides out and fill with stuffing. Then sew the opening closed.

An alternative: Fill the bears up with rice and use as boo bags.

4

5

6

7

Family SERVICE SCAVENGER HUNT

Nothing brings a family together quite like service. And what could be more fun than a scavenger hunt? For this activity we are combining the two! Use the tear-out design (page 143) to do an acts-of-service scavenger hunt with your family around your neighborhood. Bring a pen or pencil and visit your neighbors. Let them know that you are looking for a way to serve them and present them with a list of options for them to choose from for how your family can help out. After you're finished, cross off the item they chose and move on to the next house. Make it a fun event—encourage positive attitudes and kindness throughout. Your family and neighbors will talk about it for years to come!

NOTE: One of the items is to bring treats. Use a favorite family recipe or one of the recipes in this book to make treats ahead of time. Deliver to someone special, then have your children check it off the list.

NEIGHBOR MEAL

Moving into a new neighborhood can seem overwhelming. Make a new neighbor or member of your church/congregation feel welcome by inviting them over to your home for dinner. If you don't have any new neighbors moving in, you can use this as an opportunity to get to know your neighbors better. Invite them over and enjoy this meal together!

If your neighbors aren't open to the idea of coming to your home for dinner, another option is to make this meal and deliver it to them!

MEXICAN CHICKEN SOUP

This simple soup hits the spot. It doesn't take much effort but everyone who tries it loves it.

INGREDIENTS

1 chicken breast, cooked and shredded

1 can chicken broth

1 cup (186 g) cooked rice

½ cup (120 ml) salsa

OPTIONAL TOPPINGS

Shredded cheddar or jack cheese

Sour cream

1 avocado, sliced

INSTRUCTIONS

Combine the chicken, broth, rice and salsa and warm. Add any of the toppings that you'd like. Add in the jack cheese rice balls (recipe follows) for even more flair!

SIMPLE ACT ALTERNATIVE

Welcome your new neighbors to the neighborhood by writing a note on a card with some of your favorite local things. You can include restaurants, doctors, dentists, cleaners or anything local that you think might help someone new to the neighborhood.

Include your name and phone number, and encourage them to get in touch just for fun, or if they ever need some help.

JACK CHEESE RICE BALLS

These rice balls are from my good friend Kristen. She gave me this recipe years ago, and it adds something extra to this awesome soup. Yum!

INGREDIENTS

1½ cups (279 g) cooked white rice

1½ cups (350 ml) sour cream

½ lb (230 g) shredded jack cheese

½ can (4 oz [113 g]) green chopped chiles

Salt and pepper to taste

INSTRUCTIONS

Mix all of the ingredients together. Roll into golf-ball-sized rounds. Bake on a cookie sheet at 350°F (175°C) for 30 minutes. Add to Mexican Chicken Soup.

LOVE NOTES

Surprising your family and friends with love notes will make them feel thought of and appreciated. Take the opportunity to show those you care about that you think about them often.

Use the supplied love notes tear-out design (page 145) to write down what you are feeling and stick them in a lunch box, on the dashboard of the car, in a dresser drawer or somewhere unexpected.

"Guard well within yourself that treasure, kindness. Know how to give without hesitation, how to lose without regret, how to acquire without meanness."
—George Sand

FUN MAIL

With a lot of things online now, usually my mailbox is full of bills. Yuck! Did you know that you could send different sized objects through the mail? How much fun would it be to receive a flip-flop in your mailbox instead of more boring old bills?

While there are standard regulations for mail, you can send unique items from the post office. Use a printed label or a permanent marker to write the address and stick surprises in the mail. The price to ship them will depend on size and weight.

Here's a list of fun things to surprise your family and friends with:

* Message in a bottle
* Frisbee
* Seashell
* Rock (paint on the rock!)
* Box of candy
* Plastic shovel
* Coconut
* Orange
* Flip-flop
* Ball (all different types)

NOTE: Check with your local post office before attempting to mail each item.

To My Favorite Cousin
Annie Smith
1234 Sunshine Way
Happy, CA. 98765
Happy Summer!
Annie Smith
1234 Sunshine Way
Happy, CA.
98765

KINDNESS IS LIKE A BOOMERANG-
it always returns.

CHECKOUT LINE

After the first year of doing random acts of kindness for my special guy, I decided that we needed to keep it going. For his 14th birthday I set out on another mission to make the day brighter by doing random acts of kindness.

I went to the store and filled up my cart with what I needed—my normal supply of groceries and essentials for our home. I added a card to my purchases and looked around to find a checkout lane that looked empty. My heart pounded as it got closer to the end, and I was ready to pay. I started, "It's my son's birthday today. He is hard to buy for, so we are doing random acts of kindness for him. I'd like to leave this gift card for someone today. Look for a person who could really use it throughout the day."

The cashier was speechless and started to cry as I talked about J. She told me that she had two children with special needs and that she was really touched by what we were doing for him. I handed her a card that talked a little bit about him and asked her to give it to the recipient she chose for the gift card. She agreed and was excited.

I went on with my other random acts of kindness for his birthday. To my surprise, I received an email later the next day. It was from the gift card receiver. She had just started a new job as an aide in a special day class and was new to the area. Tears fell once again as I read her email. It had definitely gone to the right person.

—Mique Provost

GIFT CARDS *on* THE GO

There have been plenty of times in my life when I saw someone in need, but I wasn't really sure how to help.

Next time you are at the store, take a minute to pick out as many gift cards as you can.

Use the provided gift card tear-out design (page 147) to cheer someone up, help someone out or to pass along for fun.

Fold into 3 sections and adhere gift cards into the middle of the sleeve. Keep them on hand (in your wallet or purse), ready to help when the need arises.

NOTE: Unsure of how to go about giving out the gift cards? It can feel a little bit awkward to approach someone that you don't know. There are several ways to go about handing them out. You can leave the gift card with a worker at a store and let them pass it out to someone in need. You can leave a gift card anonymously at someone's front door or at their car. Or you can go with a more direct approach and start a conversation. Before you leave, hand the gift card over and wish the recipient a happy day.

"Real generosity is doing something nice for someone who will never find out."
—Frank A. Clark

COLORING BOOKS *for* THE EMERGENCY ROOM

Ending up in the emergency room is never a pleasant experience. It can be especially hard if you are forced to wait for hours. With this simple random act of kindness, you will brighten a child's day in a difficult time.

SUPPLIES NEEDED

Coloring books

Tear-out design (page 149)

Crayons

Pens

Basket

Bow or baker's twine

INSTRUCTIONS

Gather the supplies together. Attach the Color Your Heart Out tear-out design inside the front cover of the coloring books. You can add a small personal note or have your child handwrite something, too.

Package everything up in a basket. Tie with a bow or baker's twine and deliver to your local emergency room or urgent care.

Go to the front desk and let workers know that you have some supplies to give to kids who visit. If they can't take them there, they will tell you the best place to deliver them and direct you where to go.

"Kindness is the golden chain by which society is bound together."
—Johann Wolfgang Von Goethe

PLAY DOUGH
for PRESCHOOL

Not only is this a way to get your kids involved in a fun project that benefits other kids, your children also get to spend time in the kitchen with you! They will learn important cooking skills while making something special for someone else.

This recipe comes from my old church group and has been used for years for the toddlers and preschool age kids.

Make a batch, or several batches, to be delivered to local preschools, home day care centers or church groups.

SUPPLIES NEEDED

1 cup (120 g) flour

1 package unsweetened drink mix or food coloring of your choice (I recommend Kool-Aid)

¼ cup (75 g) salt

2 tbsp (18 g) cream of tartar

1 cup (240 ml) water

1 tbsp (15 ml) vegetable oil

INSTRUCTIONS

Mix the first four ingredients in a pan. If you don't have unsweetened drink mix or would rather not use it, you can add in about 15 drops of food coloring of your choice. Add the water and oil. Heat over medium heat for about 3–5 minutes, until the dough starts pulling away from the pan. Remove from the heat and knead until it is well combined and soft to the touch. Store in an airtight container.

NOTE: Check with the teacher of the class or group you'd like to donate the play dough to first. There could be allergy concerns or additional details to consider.

FAVORITE COOKIES
for A FAVORITE TEACHER

Let your child surprise his or her favorite teacher with a batch of cookies to let the teacher know just how much you appreciate all of the hard work.

THE BEST CHOCOLATE CHIP COOKIES EVER

Our family loves to spend time together in the kitchen baking. We have made this chocolate chip recipe over and over and over again. It's simple and tastes delicious. It's also the perfect treat to whip up for someone *just because*.

INGREDIENTS

1 cup (240 g) softened butter

1 cup (180 g) packed dark brown sugar

¾ cup (150 g) granulated sugar

2 eggs

1 tbsp (15 ml) vanilla

3 cups (360 g) flour

¾ tsp salt

¾ tsp baking soda

2 cups (340 g) milk chocolate chips

1 cup (170 g) semisweet chocolate chips

Cellophane

Twine

Tear-out design (page 151)

INSTRUCTIONS

Mix together the butter, brown sugar and granulated sugar. Stir for about 2 minutes until the mixture is well combined. Add the eggs and vanilla. Next, mix in the dry ingredients until combined. Add the chocolate chips and mix.

Bake on cookie sheets at 350°F (175°C) for 9–11 minutes. I prefer to underbake my cookies a little bit, so I do 9 minutes every time. Your cookies should be golden brown around the edges when they are ready to come out. (Oven times may vary.)

Wrap up the cookies on a plate with some cellophane and twine for the perfect touch. With your child, cut out the supplied tear-out design (page 151) and have him or her write a heartfelt note telling the teacher why your child likes being a part of his or her class.

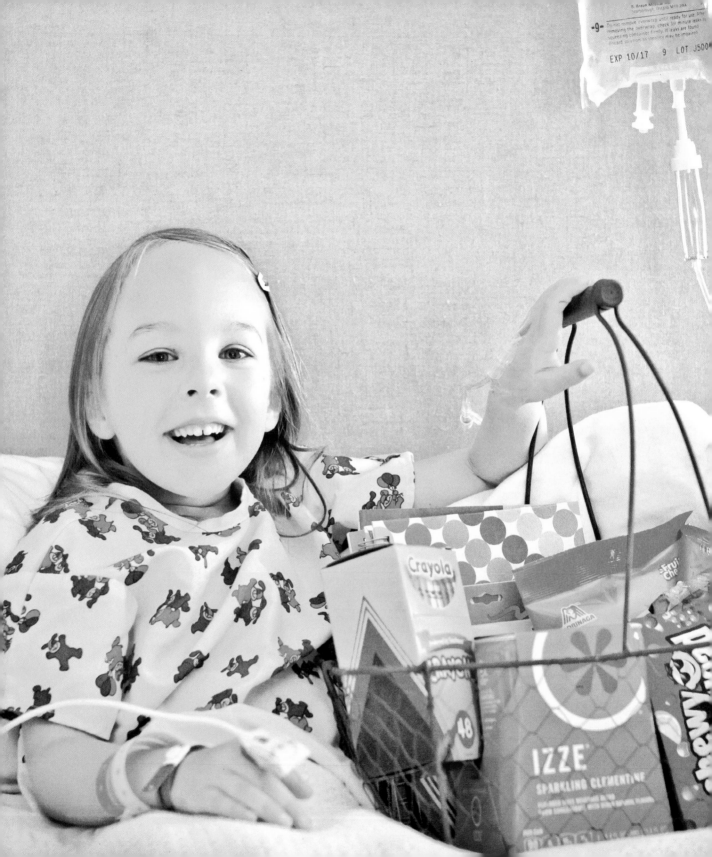

RAINBOW BOX
for HOSPITAL PATIENTS

A couple of years ago my dad was diagnosed with cancer. It was a devastating time for our family as we tried our hardest to rally around him. We had many friends and family members who brightened his tough days, as well as ours. This idea is meant to honor him, the guy who was a rainbow amongst the rain in my life. He always encouraged me to work hard, go after my dreams and find happiness when things were tough.

For this idea you will be creating a "rainbow box" to bring happiness into the lives of people who are facing challenges. Take the time to go shopping and pick out items that would make someone feel loved and appreciated.

Call your local hospital and ask if there are patients there who could use an extra dose of encouragement. Make sure that the hospital is able to accept gifts for patients before proceeding. Ask them when the best time to deliver the rainbow box would be. If you'd like to make it more of a personal connection, you can hand-deliver the box (if it is allowed). Otherwise, you can drop off the box and let the recipient receive it anonymously.

SUPPLIES NEEDED

Skittles

Magazines

Small soft blanket

Rainbow items, such as stickers, socks, bracelets, colorful drinks, etc.

Small boxes or baskets

Glue or tape

Tear-out design (page 153)

INSTRUCTIONS

The sky is the limit for this one! It will be a blast to go shopping for all kinds of fun things to put in a box of rainbows.

Gather the items together and divide them into several small boxes or baskets. Glue or tape the template from page 153 onto the top of each box. Deliver the boxes to your local hospital.

"Be a rainbow in someone else's cloud."
-Maya Angelou

HOW TO BE ENCOURAGING *in* TIMES OF TRIAL

Life was pretty good growing up. Sure, things weren't perfect, and we had our fair share of struggles. But it wasn't until I became an adult that I felt the magnitude of some pretty significant challenges. Loss of pregnancy, a child diagnosed with autism, losing my dad—all of these experiences have had a huge impact on who I am today. With each situation, I have learned more about what kind of person I'd like to be for others facing trials. Here are some ways to be encouraging to others in times of need.

LISTEN, LISTEN AND LISTEN SOME MORE.

Take time to just let the other person talk and don't respond. Take it all in. Let them get it out. This is huge to someone facing a challenge. They need to know that they are being heard. Sometimes the best support you can give is to not say a word but to listen to everything they say.

DON'T TRY TO FIX IT.

Before you go into fix-it mode, remind yourself that there are some situations that simply cannot be fixed. When people try to fix things, it sometimes makes the one grieving feel guilty or bad for feeling sad.

LET PEOPLE KNOW YOU ARE THERE FOR THEM, ALL THE TIME, WITH NO JUDGMENT.

It can be so mind numbingly hard when you are in the middle of heartache and feeling alone. Having someone to turn to, whom you know will be there under any circumstances and be loving, comforting and nonjudgmental, is the best type of medicine.

ACT.

Instead of asking how you can help, pay close attention to what the person's needs are and act on them. To make sure they are okay with it, you can say something like, "I'd like to bring you dinner. When is the best day?" Or, "I'd love to help with carpool. Who can I get in touch with?" After losing my dad, I heard, "How can I help?" so many times, but most of the time I felt like people were saying it just because they didn't know what else to say. Or they were kind of checking it off, thinking "Phew. I told her I'd help, and she didn't respond, so I did my job." Maybe that's bad of me for thinking that way, but I appreciated so much more the people who jumped in and did things without my having to even think about it. I know moving forward that that is what I will do.

ACKNOWLEDGE.

Instead of avoiding the subject with your friend/loved one, say something like "I'm so sorry that you don't have your mom to celebrate with you. That's really hard." Or, "I'm sorry. I'm sure this day is hard for you. Infertility stinks." One of the hardest things is when people don't acknowledge you problem. I think it's because they are worried they will say the wrong thing. Yes, I've done that, but I know better now. Trust me, saying nothing is usually much worse.

FOLLOW THEIR LEAD.

Everyone reacts to their situations differently. Some people completely shut down and do not want to talk about it. Others want to talk for hours. First, acknowledge the heartache, and then let them steer the conversation. If they want to talk for hours and hours, let them. If they aren't ready to really talk about it, don't push it. Let them be in charge, but be there to support them.

KNOW THAT IT IS A PROCESS.

Have you heard of the stages of grief? Well, they are real and true. Everyone experiences them in different ways and at different times. Even if you think that people should be "over" something, the pain could still very well be right on the surface. I have friends who still say that even though their mom passed away 20 years ago, they have a hard time on Mother's Day, while others spend the day celebrating with their families. Everyone experiences things differently, and it's key to know that and be aware of it. Again, take their lead after listening to them and seeing where they are.

WHEN LOSS IS EXPERIENCED, THERE IS A NEW KIND OF NORMAL.

Along with the stages of grief, when loss happens—and this applies to all different kinds of loss—things will never be the same. People learn to deal and cope without their loved one, but there is a new perspective and a spot missing for that person. Learning to live life with the loss of a dream or the loss of a parent or a child alters things.

WHAT NOT TO SAY OR DO.

In times of trial, what **not** to say is just as important as what to say or do. Good intentions can cause more hurt and pain.

Don't say, "I know how you feel," unless you actually do. Saying, "I know how you feel" can make the person dealing with loss angry (most of the anger kept inside) and want to cry out—"No you don't! You can't possibly know how I feel."

Specifically relating to loss of children, don't say, "Well at least you have another child," or something similar. A sentence started with "at least" in grieving is rarely helpful.

Don't say, "Call me," because the reality is, they won't. It's so hard to ask for help in everyday life for most people (especially women). To ask for help in dark days won't happen. Instead, you need to take the initiative and make the effort. Call them. Be there. Bring them things and do service for them.

DINNER *for* A FAMILY IN NEED

How often have you heard, "Call me if you need anything," or "Let me know if I can do anything for you." There are times when things are tough and people want to help but just aren't quite sure what to do. Instead of using those phrases, take action. Making dinner and delivering it to a friend or family in need can make someone feel loved and supported. This recipe is sure to brighten someone's day! Attach a little note (page 155) with a few words of encouragement on the back.

LASAGNA ROLL-UPS

These Lasagna Roll-Ups are a take on traditional lasagna. They are easy to put together and taste amazing. You can easily transport them and reheat at a later time.

INGREDIENTS

12 lasagna noodles

15 oz (425 g) ricotta cheese

2 cups (230 g) shredded mozzarella, divided

10 oz (280 g) frozen spinach, thawed & squeezed dry

½ cup (120 ml) sour cream

¼ cup (40 g) bread crumbs

1 tbsp (5 g) Italian seasoning

1 tsp garlic powder

15 oz (425 g) can crushed tomatoes

1½ cups (350 ml) salsa

Tear-out design (page 155)

INSTRUCTIONS

Preheat the oven to 350°F (175°C).

Cook the lasagna noodles according to the package directions and then lay them on a cookie sheet to dry a bit. Combine the ricotta, 1½ cups (172 g) of mozzarella, spinach, sour cream, bread crumbs, Italian seasoning and garlic powder to make the filling.

Spread about ⅓ cup (80 ml) of the filling down each noodle, leaving a little extra space at the end to make it stick. Roll up the noodles and place them in a 9 x 13-inch (23 x 33-cm) dish. Combine the tomatoes and salsa. Spread the mix over the roll-ups.

Bake until heated through, about 30 minutes. Immediately sprinkle with the remaining ½ cup (58 g) of mozzarella.

Cut out one of the designs on page 155 and write the recipe title and any instructions for heating it up (if needed), along with a few words of encouragement. Cover the lasagna rolls, attach the tag to the dish and deliver.

NOTE: This can be made ahead and frozen. Use a tin foil container and write instructions on how to thaw and cook when it's convenient for them on the designed tag (page 155).

"Deliberately seek opportunities for kindness, sympathy and patience."
—Evelyn Underhill

JUST BECAUSE PLATE

The great thing about doing random acts of kindness is that there doesn't have to be a reason to do them. They are random! For this project you will make a "just because" plate to pass from friend to friend. Fill it with some of your favorite treats, such as Zucchini Chocolate Bread (page 107) or The Best Chocolate Chip Cookies Ever (page 50), and deliver it to someone who will enjoy it and then make a new batch and pass it on to the next friend.

SUPPLIES NEEDED

Plate, washed and dried

Graphite stick

Plain printer paper

Tape

Tear-out design (page 157)

Pencil

Oil-based paint markers

Cookies, cupcakes or other treats

Plastic wrap or cellophane

INSTRUCTIONS

Prepare the design on the plate: Use the graphite stick to thickly color over the paper, in a circle large enough to cover the dish. Tape the paper onto the plate with the graphite side on top of the plate.

Position the tear-out design where you want the design to show up. Trace the design with the pencil, pressing firmly for a good transfer. Remove the design and paper to see how it transferred. If you don't like it you can start over!

Use your oil-based paint markers to trace over the graphite design. Let the plate dry for 24 hours.

Heat the oven to 350°F (175°C). Place the plate in the oven while it warms up. When it reaches 350°F (175°C), set the timer for 30 minutes. After 30 minutes, carefully remove the plate from the oven. This process will make your plate and the design dishwasher safe.

Fill up the plate with treats, cover with plastic wrap or cellophane and deliver.

PAY IT FORWARD

Having recently separated from my husband, I was living in small house, supporting my family all by myself working at a doctor's office. It was the holidays, and it was after the movie *Pay It Forward* had been released. I came home from work to a FedEx envelope in my mailbox. I stood there wondering what it was because I was totally broke and had not ordered anything. I opened it up and it contained the book *Pay It Forward*. I was even more confused because I certainly had not ordered that book. My natural reaction was to flip through the pages, and as I did five one-hundred dollar bills came flying out. I stood there in amazement and of course started to cry. I still have the book in the FedEx envelope.

—Lisa Arnold

LOVE AND KINDNESS
go hand in hand.

-MARIAN KEYES

KINDNESS ROCKS

Kids love to get messy and paint. Why not turn their love for creating into a random act of kindness? Decorate your community with bright and fun painted rocks; they'll definitely put a smile on someone's face.

You will first need to go on a walk to collect rocks. Help kids find flat rocks to use for this project.

SUPPLIES NEEDED

Rocks

Paint

Paintbrushes

INSTRUCTIONS

This is as simple as it gets! Gather rocks and have your child paint inspiring things on them, like rainbows, hearts or favorite sayings. Anything uplifting is game for this activity. Use the time with your kids to talk about what kindness means to you and how we can be kind to one another.

After you've finished painting the rocks together, spread them throughout your community—at a local park, in your front yard, on a walking trail, etc.

"Three things in human life are important. The first is to be kind. The second is to be kind. And the third is to be kind."
—Henry James

RANDOM ACT of KINDNESS DATE

Sometimes it can feel almost impossible to find the time for date night. But, it's oh so important. Instead of heading to a movie or a nice dinner, why not spend one night focusing on others? For this project you will compile several random acts of kindness to complete together.

Sit down as a couple before a night out and decide what you'd like to do for your random acts of kindness. The traditional small and simple random acts of kindness, found on page 13, can be used or you can write down your own ideas on the designed notes on page 159. Grab a jar to stick your options in and pull out several possibilities. You don't have to complete them all on one date but can use them for several nights out.

Pass out the included tags (page 161) as you complete each one.

FISHTAIL FRIENDSHIP BRACELETS
for THE HOSPITAL

Friendship bracelets have been around for a long time. The styles change, but the idea behind them remains the same—making something for someone you care about that represents your friendship. With this easy craft, kids will have the opportunity to create something special for children who could use a pick-me-up. You'll create friendship bracelets to deliver to a local hospital.

Make sure to give your local hospital a call and ask if there is a need for these bracelets before you get started. Oftentimes there are certain hospitals that specialize in long-term care (children included). If your hospital is not one of them, they can direct you where to go.

These instructions are for making one bracelet. When you call the hospital, you can find out how many you should make.

There are several ways that you can deliver the bracelets. They can be dropped off at the appropriate unit anonymously. Or you can bring your kids with you to let them be involved in the process. If they go to visit, have a conversation prior to arriving about the children who are sick in the hospital. In some instances, your kids will be able to hand-deliver the bracelets to the young patients. In others, they will need to give them to the nurses to pass out.

SUPPLIES NEEDED

Embroidery thread of varying colors

Safety pin or tape

Scissors

INSTRUCTIONS

You will need two strands of each desired color of thread. Cut each to the same length, approximately 2 feet (60 cm). Gather all of your thread together and tie a square knot at the top. You can either use a safety pin or tape to secure the bracelet and make it easy to braid.

Separate your threads into two sections making sure to have two strands per color on each side. Use photos on the opposite page as a guide.

Grab one color from the right side and pull it to the middle. Then pull the same color from the left side. Now add the piece from the left side and pull it over all the strands of thread to the middle. Then add it to the right side and pull the groups at the top to tighten. It'll be important to keep tightening as you move along.

Repeat this until you've gone through all of your colors.

When you've repeated until the desired length, tie a knot at the bottom.

You should have a knot at the top and a knot at the bottom with excess strands on either side to make the bracelet.

This project is meant to be simple so that kids of all ages can make them. But for a fancier, more involved look you can add beads, dangles or whatever you'd like to the bracelets.

DIY NO-SLIP SOCKS

These no-slip socks provide safety and comfort, and they are fun to put together! You only need a few things to make them.

These would be perfect for an elderly facility, nursing home, physical therapist office or hospital. They also make nice surprise gifts for little ones or a grandparent to brighten their day with kindness.

SUPPLIES NEEDED

Socks

Cardboard (optional)

Puffy paints

Gift bags (optional)

Tear-out design (page 163)

INSTRUCTIONS

Lay socks with the backsides facing up. You can place a piece of cardboard in the middle to make sure that the top and bottom layer of the sock don't get stuck together from the paint.

Use the puffy paints to make designs. Simpler designs are suggested because the puffy paint can crack over time from laundering.

Let them dry for 24 hours before delivering. Wrap them up in individual gift bags, if desired, and attach the supplied tag.

HOSPITALITY BAGS

There are millions of people who spend their days caring for the needs of others. Whether it's the mom of a special-needs child or the wife of a sick husband, there is a definite need to show support. I witnessed my mom and mother-in-law care for their husbands. I was amazed at their selfless actions and was inspired by their strength. Often caretakers are overlooked. You have the opportunity to let them know that they are not forgotten.

You can make hospitality bags for someone that you know personally who is a caretaker, or you can put together several bags and deliver them to an organization like Ronald McDonald House (http://www.rmhc .org/). Ronald McDonald House and similar organizations provide housing for families who are taking care of loved ones in hospitals away from their homes.

This project should be tailored to the specific recipient in mind. For those who are taking care of someone in the hospital, you can include hand sanitizer, warm socks, a gift card for music, lotion, a journal, crossword puzzles and a book. If you are delivering to a caretaker for someone with special needs, include a handwritten note, journal, gift card for a manicure, etc. Use your creativity and think of what would make each person feel loved and appreciated. Include a tag from the tear-out design on page 165 with each bag, and a personalized message if you'd like.

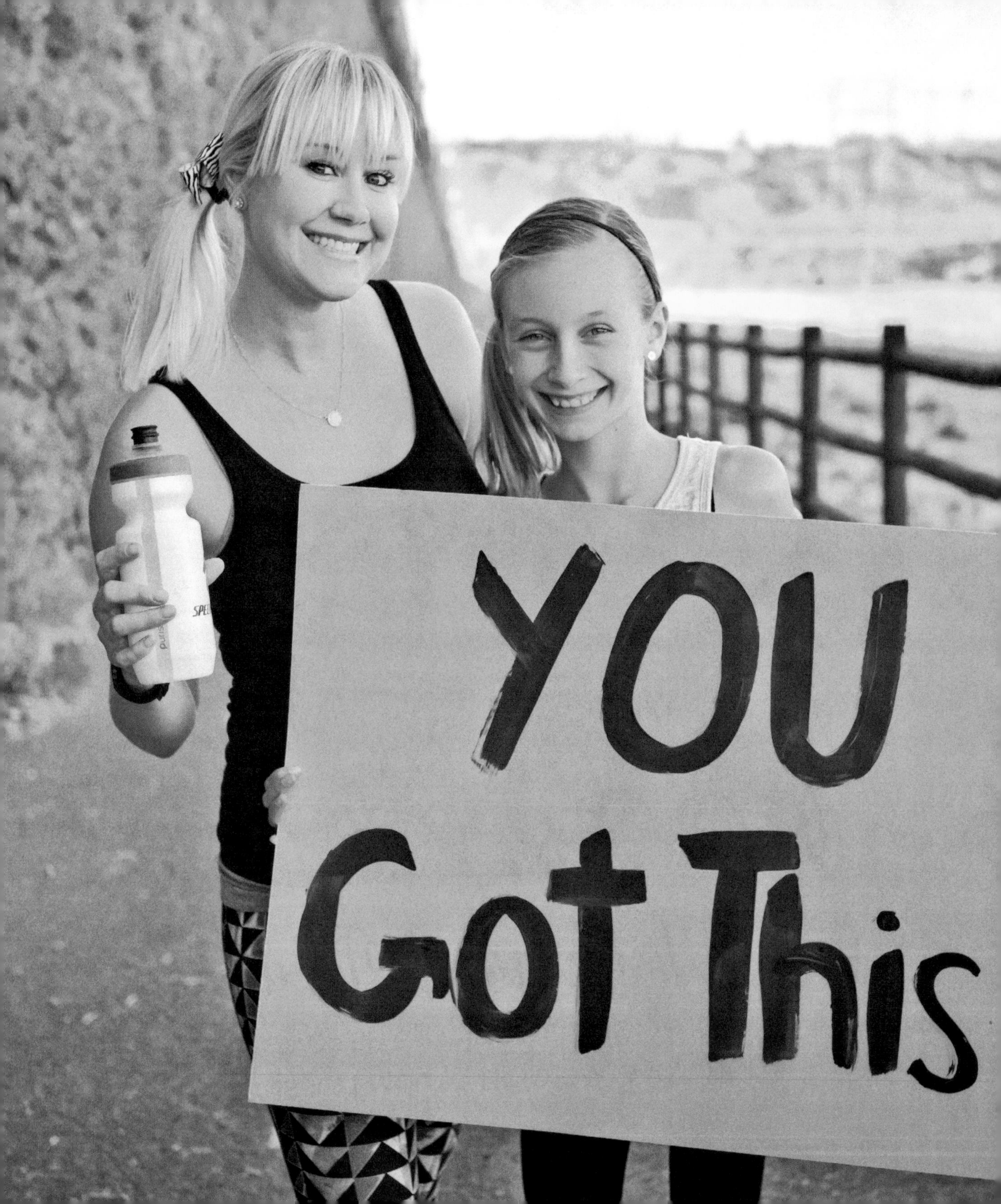
YOU
Got This

RACE-DAY SIGNS

Several years ago my sister challenged me to run a half-marathon with her. It was a big deal to train and make it to the finish line. One of the things that encouraged me the most while I was running those 13.1 miles (21 km) was the crowd of people cheering and the fun signs along the way. For this random act of kindness you will become a marathon cheerleader!

SUPPLIES NEEDED

Markers

Butcher paper or poster board

INSTRUCTIONS

All you need is a little imagination and inspiration to encourage people on race day.

Here are some suggestions for sayings:

* You can and you will.

* Pain is temporary. Pride is forever.

* No matter how slow you go, you're still lapping everyone on the couch.

* You can run, but you can't hide!

* Keep Calm and Marath-on.

BONUS IDEA: In addition to cheering on and bringing signs, there are always opportunities to volunteer for races. Get in touch with local race organizers to see how you can contribute.

"If you want to lift yourself up, lift up someone else."
—Booker T. Washington

THANK-YOU NOTES

It seems like thank-you notes are a thing of the past. Oh how Emily Post would be disappointed! Right up there with teaching kids kindness is teaching them to be appreciative and grateful. For this activity you will help them do just that—give thanks!

SUPPLIES NEEDED

Thank-you note tear-out design (page 167)

Pen/pencil

INSTRUCTIONS

Help your child think about someone who has affected his or her life for good. This could be their favorite doctor, dentist, librarian, crosswalk attendant, mail carrier or anyone they want to thank.

Kids will use the thank-you note design and write their appreciation and what he or she means to them.

Have a conversation about the importance of thanking people and recognizing people in our lives that serve.

BUSY BAGS *for* LITTLE ONES

People always said that time would fly by and that my kids would be big before I knew it. I laughed because when they were little the days were long. Somehow time has indeed flown by, and now, before I know it, they will be out of my house. But I still vividly remember all of the activities that I came up with to keep my kids entertained. My sister, Jessica, is in the thick of things with little ones and recently put together a group with her friends to exchange busy bags. These bags are just like they sound—they are meant to help keep kids busy. They can be used at home, at doctor's appointments or on a long car ride.

Use this idea to create a group, like my sister did, or to make and donate to a homeless shelter or a doctor's office. There are a lot of different ways that this can be transformed into a random act of kindness to benefit kids and their parents. There are all kinds of busy bags that you can make, but here is a super simple idea that doubles as an educational activity.

SUPPLIES NEEDED

Self-adhesive Velcro dots

Colored craft sticks

Zip pencil pouch

Tear-out designs (page 169)

INSTRUCTIONS

Add self-adhesive Velcro dots to the ends of the colored craft sticks. Slide the sticks into the zip pencil pouch with one or both of the tear-out designs.

Kids can use the tear-out design as a guide to create shapes, letters, numbers and more with the Velcro craft sticks. For younger kids, you will need to show them that the sticks attach with the Velcro at the ends. Older kids can create more elaborate shapes and designs.

SPREAD LOVE
EVERYWHERE YOU GO.
LET NO ONE COME
TO YOU WITHOUT
leaving happier.

-BLESSED MOTHER TERESA

MAKEUP COUNTER TREAT

I was newly married and in a new city. I had just met a girl at our church. She mentioned that she worked at a makeup counter at a department store. I gushed over how much I loved a particular eye shadow from that company.

A few weeks later, I came home from a long day at work and found a little mint green box tied with a bow inside my door. It was my favorite eye shadow! I loved getting the eye shadow for free, but even more that she had listened and remembered the exact shade that I liked.

Because of this kind gesture, I now love leaving treats for friends and neighbors just for fun on their doorsteps.

—Alissa Udy

ENCOURAGING KINDNESS
in THE SPECIAL-NEEDS COMMUNITY

When I was in high school I took a psychology class. We studied all kinds topics for that subject, but the one thing I really remember was helping in the special day class. When we first started working with that class I was nervous. I didn't know what to say or do, but the more time I spent, the less intimidated I became.

In college I worked in a mailroom with two volunteers who had special needs. They were passionate about their work and fun to be around. I then got a job at a school as a teacher's aide for two kids who had Down syndrome. All of these experiences shaped who I am as a person and as a mother.

My son was diagnosed with autism over 13 years ago. A lot has changed since his diagnosis. I have learned a lot about autism. I have also learned a ton about how to treat (or not to treat) people with special needs.

If you lead with kindness, you can't go wrong. But here are some suggestions on interacting with those who have special needs:

FIRST AND FOREMOST, DON'T BE AFRAID TO ASK QUESTIONS.

I love when people ask me questions about my son J, or autism in general. To me it says that they want to get to know him, and I'd much rather have people ask than wonder or assume. I think it goes without saying that questions asked should be appropriate in nature. As much as I love answering questions, I'd rather not address a question like, "So it must really stink having a child with autism, huh?" Instead ask things like "What does J like to do these days?" or "What's he learning about at school?" or the best one, "How can I help?"

KNOW THAT CHILDREN WITH SPECIAL NEEDS ARE ALL DIFFERENT FROM EACH OTHER.

Not all kids with autism don't make eye contact, can count cards and avoid being around people. In fact, most are not like that. Each child has his or her own set of challenges and strengths. Take the time to get to know the person—what they like and don't like. Each person with special needs has varying limitations; some children will be able to communicate well while others are severely impacted and struggle to speak at all.

DON'T BE INTIMIDATED.

As I mentioned, the first distinct memories I have of interacting with someone with special needs was in high school. I was nervous. I didn't know what to do or how I should act. What if I did it wrong? But all it took was a little bit of time with the kids and my fears went away. It can be the same way for you. Even though each child is different, try to find a way to engage the child. If you know he/she likes trains, ask about trains. If there is no response, try approaching it in a different way—point out a train and ask specific questions. Most kids with special needs do better with visual cues and specific questions. If you are trying to get them to do something, model it for them. Have them imitate you. Say "try this," and show them. My biggest advice is to just keep trying. Don't miss out on the chance to get to know a really amazing person just because you don't think you can get through. There is always a way—you just might have to get creative in your approach.

TRY NOT TO TALK DOWN.

It's sad when I hear people talk to my J really slowly and really loudly. I understand that they speak to him like that because they are unsure of how to talk to him. And sometimes (most times) he doesn't respond when a question is asked of him. But that doesn't mean he doesn't understand. If you are unsure of how much the child you are talking to will understand, ask his or her parents for advice.

OFFER TO HELP, INSTEAD OF HURT.

I can't count how many times I've been out and about with J and people have stared or done a double take at seeing him. Usually it's because he is sucking his thumb (at 15), flapping his hands or having a meltdown. I, as his mother, am fully aware that his behavior is not appropriate. The last thing I need/want is for everyone in a store to stare me down, whisper under their breath or say hurtful things aloud. Instead, smile. It's simple but can make an overwhelmed mom who is trying her very hardest feel less judged. Along with that, know that children with special needs aren't "bad" and often have a really hard time controlling their behaviors.

HAVE A CONVERSATION WITH YOUR KIDS.

Starting at a young age, teach your kids that it's okay to be different. If you're not sure exactly how to start a conversation, point out something about them that sets them apart. Highlight how cool it is that they have three freckles on their face and how that makes them unique. Explain how boring it would be if every person looked and acted the same. You can then bridge the conversation to how important it is to realize that just because someone learns or acts differently, that they are still worthwhile. All kids need to know that just because Ryan doesn't play the same way or that Adam reacts differently to a situation, that they are still a person with a place in this world. If you know that you'll be around someone with special needs beforehand (a playdate, for example), talk to your kids about what they can expect or what to anticipate. And once you get there, be the example. Your children look to you to know how to act. If you act in a loving, understanding, kind and accepting way, they will follow your lead.

WEIGHTED BAGS
for SPECIAL DAY CLASS

We have experienced many special day classes over the years. While there are challenges, you would be hard-pressed to find a classroom more full of joy than a special-needs class. Often in these classes there are children with sensory disorders or those who have sensory needs. Making weighted bags for the kids in a class will make them feel thought of and can help with sensory issues.

SUPPLIES NEEDED

Fabric—standard size for this is 12 x 12 inches (30 x 30 cm)

Rice

Sewing machine or needle and thread

INSTRUCTIONS

Fold the fabric in half, with the right sides (the pretty side) together.

Leaving a ¾-inch (2-cm) seam allowance, sew (with machine or by hand) straight lines around the bag. Make sure to leave a 1–2-inch (2.5–5-cm) opening to have a spot to fill the rice.

Flip the bag inside out and add the rice inside.

You want it be full enough to have weight but not be too full.

Sew the opening closed (again, by hand or with a machine).

You can take this same idea and make a weighted blanket with more materials.

NOTE: Get in touch with your local school and/or school district to ask which class(es) could benefit most from these weighted bags.

HUGS & KISSES

Let the people you care about know just how much they are loved with this easy project. You will gather a few simple supplies and create bags of "Hugs and Kisses" to hang from the doorknob as a surprise.

SUPPLIES NEEDED

Small chocolate pieces (I recommend Hershey's Hugs and Kisses)

Other favorite candies

Cellophane

Ribbon

Mini bells

Tear-out hugs and kisses design (page 171)

INSTRUCTIONS

Get packages of small chocolates and favorite candies from the store. Cut the cellophane into squares. Lay out a handful of the candies in the middle of the cellophane. Bring the sides of the cellophane up to meet in the middle. Wrap ribbon around the treat. Then make one big loop to be able to hang the bag from a doorknob. Tie it onto the first ribbon. Finally, tie on mini bells so that when the door is opened they will hear the bells and be reminded that they were thought of! Add tag.

If you're feeling bold, go ahead and leave a bag anonymously on the door of a neighbor with an inspirational quote on the tag, just because.

BOOKMARKS *for* THE LIBRARY

When my kids were little we spent time in our local library checking out new books, seeing what movies they had to offer and just getting out of our everyday routine!

For this activity you will have your kids donate books to the library and include bookmarks to surprise the recipient with!

Gather books that are in great condition that you no longer use (or purchase new books) to donate. Color the tear-out bookmarks on page 173 and write a message on them. Stick one inside each book to make the person who receives it feel special!

DING DONG DONUTS

This random act of kindness is one you can do for anyone. Pick up a box of your favorite donuts. Attach the tear-out design (page 175) and deliver the donuts. Ring the doorbell and run so that the receiver can have a surprise waiting for them when they open their door.

Half of the fun is in knowing that you dropped off a delicious treat and that they will never know who was thinking of them. It'll be your little secret!

CREAM PUFFS *for* COMMUNITY HELPERS

My mom made these cream puffs for my family, and they were always a favorite! You can help lift someone up and bring a smile to his or her face by making a plate of these to deliver. Some suggestions for who to deliver to—postal or delivery workers, sanitary employees, librarians, nurses or anyone in the community that you'd like to honor.

CREAM PUFFS

These cream puffs are light and fluffy. Finish them off with your favorite pudding mix and drizzle with chocolate or powdered sugar. Delicious!

INGREDIENTS

1 cup (120 g) flour

¼ tsp salt

½ cup (120 g) butter

1 cup (240 ml) boiling water

4 eggs

1 package pudding mix of your choice (I prefer vanilla)

4 oz (113 g) cream cheese, softened

Melted chocolate or raspberry jam to drizzle (optional)

Powdered sugar (optional)

INSTRUCTIONS

Preheat oven to 425°F (218°C).

Sift the flour and salt. Melt the butter in the boiling water in a medium saucepan over low heat. Add the flour all at once and stir with a whisk continuously, until the mixture forms a ball and leaves the side of the pan. Cook another two minutes on low until the mixture is dry. Remove from the heat.

Add the eggs one at a time. Beat the mixture after each addition. A whisk or electric mixer can be used for this part. Continue beating until a thick dough forms.

Drop rounded tablespoons onto a parchment-paper-lined baking sheet, 2 inches (5 cm) apart.

Place in the oven and bake for 15 minutes. Reduce the heat to 400°F (205°C), and bake another 15 minutes. Reduce again to 375°F (190°C), and bake 10 more minutes, or until moisture beads no longer appear on the surface of the puffs. This should be approximately 40 minutes total baking time. Don't open the oven to check during the baking time.

Remove to a wire rack to cool. When cool, cut the top off of puffs and remove the centers. Make the pudding according to the directions on the package. Add the softened cream cheese and mix until fully combined. Fill the cream puffs with pudding mix. You can use any other type of filling you'd like—different kinds of pudding, whipped cream, etc.

Drizzle with the melted chocolate or raspberry jam, or sprinkle with powdered sugar to finish.

To deliver these yummy treats in the freshest way, bring them to community workers on a cute serving plate with plastic wrap. Airtight recyclable containers are another great idea. If you want to take it one step further, add an uplifting note to delivery.

FLAGS
for VETERANS

Every Memorial Day, Veterans Day and 4th of July we see flags lining our streets in support of our troops and in celebration of our country. But there are another 362 days a year to pay our respects and show our support to veterans who now serve or have served in the past. This idea can be done in addition to the Letters to Troops (page 177).

SUPPLIES NEEDED

Tear-out design (page 177)

Hole punch

Mini flag

Twine, string or yarn to attach card

INSTRUCTIONS

Use the tear-out design to write a heartfelt note to a veteran. Make sure that they know how much you appreciate their service to our country. Using a hole punch, create a hole to attach the note to the flag with twine, string or yarn and stick the flag in their yard.

"Kindness in words creates confidence. Kindness in thinking creates profoundness. Kindness in giving creates love."
—Lao Tzu

Kindness
IS THE LANGUAGE
WHICH THE DEAF
CAN HEAR & THE
BLIND CAN SEE.

-MARK TWAIN

BIRTHDAY KINDNESS

On my 28th birthday, I went around Okinawa, Japan, and did 28 random acts of kindness. At the end of the day, I had 27 completed, and we were just around the corner from my house. I had made little airplanes out of Smarties, Life Savers and gum so I hopped out of the car and went to my neighbor's house. She's a lovely woman with a mentally disabled son. We'd exchanged waves and smiles on our way to and from work, but neither of us spoke the same language, so I don't even know her name and she doesn't know mine. However, when I gave her son the candy airplane, they were both so happy and excited. There was no need to be able to speak the same language because, in that moment, we were both feeling the same emotions—joy and gratitude.

—Kassie O'Driscoll

BIRTHDAY RANDOM ACTS *of* KINDNESS

My love and passion for random acts of kindness came from the birthday gift I gave to my son then turning 13 years old. It was the best way to spend a day celebrating him.

In order to pull off a day of birthday random acts of kindness you need a little bit of time to plan. There are several ways to go about it. You can do it every hour throughout the day. You can do as many as the year that they are turning (13 acts for 13 years, etc.). You can do as many as the day will allow. Refer to the traditional small and simple acts of kindness on page 13 for a place to start planning.

One of the fun things that came of our day celebrating J was having other family and friends join in the festivities. Recruit the people you love to be involved and make it even more memorable.

Use the tear-out design on page 179 to attach to things along the way!

"Everyone responds to kindness."
-Richard Gere

GAMES
at AN ELDERLY FACILITY

My mother-in-law is the ultimate example of caring for the elderly. She has a talent for being a good friend and an uplifting person around those who need her. One thing I've learned from her is that spending time with someone is sometimes the best thing you can do for him or her.

Taking your kids to an elderly facility will not only help those you visit feel special and cared about, but will also help younger generations learn a lot from their elders.

There are a number of things you can do to spend quality time, but one simple suggestion is to play games.

This project will be most successful by calling ahead and checking in with the senior center. Ask them for the most ideal time to visit and bring games with your kids. There are often visiting hours—times that are designated for people to visit. You also might be able to get specific information about guests' favorite games and activities.

SUPPLIES NEEDED

Card games

Clothespins

Markers

INSTRUCTIONS

My kids love playing card games. They especially like playing "Hand & Foot" and "Knock" with their grandma.

You can either decorate your clothespins prior to visiting the facility or bring the supplies to make them fancy there.

The clothespins are used to hold cards in delicate hands.

"That best portion of a man's life, his little, nameless, unremembered acts of kindness and love."
—William Wordsworth

Little FREE LIBRARY

I was introduced to the idea of a "free library" recently and fell in love with it. It not only encourages reading but also sharing and a sense of community. There is a website dedicated to this idea called the Little Free Library (http://littlefreelibrary.org/). People from all over have created libraries in front of their homes with signs that let visitors know to take a book and/or leave a book. Some have themes; others are simple. And the idea is all based around the love of reading.

You can use the building plans and blueprints on the Little Free Library website or go searching for your own ideas. I have a dollhouse that I bought at our local antique mall a few years ago. I knew it'd be an awesome starting point for a free library.

Use the supplied sign (page 181) to attach to your own free library and spread random acts of kindness throughout the year with books.

Encouraging
SIDEWALK ART

Get busy crafting to make this easy chalk paint and use it to spread the love. This is a great activity to get your kids outside, using their creativity to inspire and encourage others.

SUPPLIES NEEDED

¼ cup (30 g) cornstarch

¼ cup (60 ml) water

Food coloring

Paintbrushes

INSTRUCTIONS

This is the recipe that you will need for each color. It is equal parts cornstarch to water, so if you'd like to make more of each color, simply double or triple the amounts.

Whisk the cornstarch with the water until all the clumps are gone. Add drops of food coloring until you get the intensity of color you want. Fill the cups of a muffin tin with different colors of the sidewalk chalk paint. Grab your paintbrushes and head outdoors!

Choose areas in your community to color, draw and make someone's day. This could be at the park, on a walking trail, for a neighbor or a family member who lives close by, etc. If you choose a walking or running area, painting sayings like, "You can do it" or "You're almost there" will really be encouraging to those who run past it.

LUNCH BOX NOTES

I know, I know—it's hard enough to put together lunch on most days. At least that's how it is at our house. But taking less than one minute to add sweet lunch box notes into your kids' lunches will make them feel extra loved and thought of.

Simply cut out the lunch box notes on page 183, add a little message on the backside and stick it in your child's lunch box.

SIMPLE ACT ALTERNATIVE

Use a dry erase marker to write an encouraging note on your kids' bathroom mirror. This will start their day off on the right foot before heading to school and can be easily erased later.

"A little spark of kindness can put a colossal burst of sunshine into someone's day."
—Unknown

ZUCCHINI CHOCOLATE BREAD

Throughout this book I've shared several ideas that involve treats. Making treats is my way of showing love! My mom shared this recipe with me, and it is not only delicious but easy to make. Give a loaf (or two!) of this home-baked sweet bread to a friend in need of a pick-me-up, a neighbor or even a stranger and let them know they are special.

This recipe would be great to use for the Family Scavenger Hunt (page 35) or the Just Because Plate (page 59).

INGREDIENTS

2 cups (400 g) sugar

1 cup (218 g) coconut oil

3 eggs

½ cup (117 ml) sour cream (plain yogurt can be used instead)

1 tbsp (15 ml) vanilla extract

2½ cups (300 g) all-purpose flour

½ cup (55 g) powder cocoa

1 tsp salt

1 tsp baking soda

¼ tsp baking powder

1 tsp ground cinnamon

2 cups (340 g) shredded zucchini

1 cup (180 g) semisweet chocolate chips

INSTRUCTIONS

Preheat the oven to 350°F (175°C).

In a large bowl, blend the sugar, oil, eggs, sour cream and vanilla until well mixed. Combine the dry ingredients separately and gradually beat the dry mixture into the sugar mixture. Blend in the shredded zucchini and finally the chocolate chips.

Pour into two greased loaf pans. Bake for 50–55 minutes, or until a toothpick inserted into the center of the bread comes out clean.

IT'S NICE TO
BE IMPORTANT,
BUT IT'S MORE
IMPORTANT TO
be nice.

-JOHN TEMPLETON

POCKET FULL OF KINDNESS

We were taking the kids camping for a long weekend in the summer. My husband had to work late, so I had all three girls with me alone. We stopped for gas in a small town on the way to our campsite. I went into the store to pay and pick up some water. The kids had stayed in the car. When I came back out they had locked the doors to the car. I went to open them and the alarm went off before I could press the unlock button.

In all this confusion I left my wallet on top of the car. I forgot my wallet was up there and took off for the campsite.

I got the tent all set up and got the girls in bed when I got a phone call from a number I didn't recognize. Then the number texted me, and it was my eye doctor of all people. He said that someone had found my wallet, and his card was in it so they called him. I called the woman who found my wallet, and she was very kind. She and her son were going to go get ice cream, and they saw my wallet on the side of the road. They then went around and picked up all the cards and everything that fell out when I took off from the gas station. My husband stopped by this woman's house to pick up my wallet. I am still ever so grateful for this act of kindness. She didn't have to stop and wander around on the side of the road to find my belongings, but she did.

—Liz Hedenland

FRUIT DIP
for COWORKERS

Chances are you spend a lot of time with the people you work with daily, right? Why not surprise them with a little treat out of the blue? You can show how much you appreciate them with this simple and delicious fruit dip.

CARAMEL APPLE DIP

This dip is one of my favorites from my mom. It's hard to eat just one bite!

INGREDIENTS

½ stick (¼ cup [60 g]) butter

¾ cup (135 g) brown sugar

8 oz (226 g) cream cheese, at room temperature

1 tsp vanilla

Pinch of salt

Sliced apples or other fruit

INSTRUCTIONS

Melt the butter and brown sugar together in a covered dish in the microwave on high for 1 minute. Stir the mixture with a whisk. Stir in the cream cheese. Add the vanilla and salt.

Serve with apples and other fruit.

"I always say that kindness is the greatest beauty that you can have."
—Andie MacDowell

INSPIRATIONAL QUOTES

I have collected quotes since I was in junior high. I love reading them and posting them in visible places so I can continue to be inspired. Why not spread some sunshine by sharing quotes to uplift others?

SUPPLIES NEEDED

Tear-out quotes (pages 185–187)

Scissors

Tape

Envelopes

INSTRUCTIONS

Simply cut out the quotes and use the tape to secure them where others will find them. You can send these quotes in the mail to someone in need, or deliver them to teachers or firefighters or to the library—any person or place that you think could use a little encouragement! You could tape them to bathroom mirrors, pin them to a community board or anywhere else that is noticeable.

"The smallest act of kindness is worth more than the grandest intention."

—Oscar Wilde

LEMONADE STAND
with A TWIST

Every summer, lemonade stands pop up with cute kids trying to raise money. Instead of raising money to use on a new toy, use this idea to encourage kids to raise funds for someone in need or a charity close to their heart. You can help them make signs and set up shop in your front yard or on the sidewalk. Use the time to teach the importance of generosity and kindness to your children. And people in your community will certainly be inspired as well!

FRUIT JUICE SPRITZERS

You only need a few ingredients to take a drink from boring to fabulous—and these fruity spritzers are definitely fabulous! The key to making these drinks is several flavors of fruit juice, sparkling water for fizz and crushed ice to keep them cool and refreshing.

PINEAPPLE ORANGE

3 cups (700 ml) chilled pineapple juice

1 cup (240 ml) chilled orange juice

Crushed ice cubes

2 cups (475 ml) sparkling water

INSTRUCTIONS

Mix chilled pineapple juice and orange juice in a pitcher.

Put crushed ice into a glass and pour the juice mix into the glasses, about two-thirds of the way.

Add the sparkling water to the glass.

BERRY LEMON LIME

1 bag frozen mixed berries

3 cups (700 ml) chilled lemonade

1 cup (240 ml) chilled limeade

Crushed ice cubes

2 cups (475 ml) sparkling water

INSTRUCTIONS

Combine berries with lemonade and limeade in a pitcher and mix well.

Put crushed ice into a glass and pour the juice mix over the ice.

Add the sparkling water to the glass and stir.

Mini FIRST AID KIT

With this easy project you can make a big impact in a short amount of time. You will put together mini first aid kits to donate to homeless shelters or local organizations in need. Contact your local shelters, schools, first responders or organizations that would benefit most from first aid kids. Because they are mini, they can easily be added to backpacks or used for travel.

Buying the items in bulk and dividing them into a large amount of kits will help keep the price down and allow you to put more together. Gather the needed supplies and assemble the kits with friends and family. Remember to include the kids as they can easily help and will see firsthand how their service impacts a community.

SUPPLIES NEEDED

Tear-out design (page 189)

Clear plastic soap containers

Bandages

Travel-size packs of antibacterial wipes

Cotton swabs

Mini bottles of hand sanitizer

Gauze

INSTRUCTIONS

To put these kits together use the provided First Aid Kit tear-out design and slide it into the inside of the soap container. Add the first aid supplies and close.

SHARE *the* BOUNTY

If you have a green thumb, this is the perfect random act of kindness for you!

My mom always made our gardens beautiful at our home. Unfortunately, I didn't inherit her green thumb, but that makes me appreciate her talent all the more. My parents built their dream home with raised garden beds for fruit and vegetables. It is gorgeous and full of amazing food. She gives away fresh fruit and vegetables often, as she's unable to eat it all before it goes bad.

With this act of kindness, sharing comes full circle. You can share the bounty of your garden and invite others to share from theirs as well!

SUPPLIES NEEDED

Tear-out design (page 191)

Basket, bucket, box or other container

Fresh items from your garden, such as flowers, fruit or vegetables

INSTRUCTIONS

Putting together the basket is simple—use the tear-out design as a sign to attach to the basket (or other container) and fill it up with items from your garden.

Either deliver the basket to someone or leave it somewhere as a surprise. They can enjoy your excess and return it to give some of their extra produce when they have it. Like the Just Because Plate (page 59), it could even become a traveling basket of garden goods!

PASSING ON THE TRADITION

When we lived in Florida and would need to cross the Sunshine Skyway in or out of Tampa, I always made it a point to carry a few extra dollars and would pay the toll for the next car behind me. Our daughter loved it so much. She'd ask as we got closer, "Are we paying for someone else today?" and then would happily pull out the money and hand it to the toll worker.

Anytime there is a toll road, I try my best to include extra to cover at least one car behind me. (This works only when paying in cash at the toll booths.) My mother once paid for five cars when we spent an afternoon in Chicago. Seeing her do it inspired me to do it when I was older, and now I've passed that fun on to my own daughter.

—Le Ann Hall

CONCLUSION

Remember how I mentioned at the beginning of this book about it being a jumping-off point? Now that you've made it to the end of the book, I hope it has given you ideas and empowered you to jump out of your comfort zone to help others in meaningful ways.

No matter where you are or what you have going on, there are little opportunities to serve those around you every day. Before long you realize that the little things are actually the big things. By doing random acts of kindness, you are making a difference in your heart, your home, your community and the world. When we join together and actively spread love, amazing things can happen. I've seen it. I hope you will see it, too.

ACKNOWLEDGMENTS

Thank you to the team at Page Street Publishing who believed in this book and gave me the opportunity to see my vision through.

A huge thanks to Alyssa Bazar for the beautiful photography and styling, which made my ideas come to life.

Thank you to my family who has not only supported me in this adventure but in every adventure—the happiest of happy times, the hardest of hard times and everything in between. To my creative and determined mom, Syndea, my patient and loving dad, Randy, sister and best friend Jessica, thoughtful brother Tony and their cute spouses and kids. To my mother-in-law Yvonne who is an example of giving of herself, always. Thank you to the many friends who have become family to me and encouraged me throughout this process.

And to my Jonathan, Julia and Andrew—the three that make me crazy proud and sometimes crazy frustrated too. I love you more than you'll ever know. I hope you are always inspired to be kind and brave. Thank you to Josh for being my biggest supporter and for making me laugh every day—even when I think I don't want to. You are everything to me.

ABOUT THE AUTHOR

With her creative blog, Thirty Handmade Days, Mique Provost spends her time inspiring others to create. Cheerful printables, easy-to-fix recipes, organizing and parenting ideas plus unique but simple gift ideas can all be found daily on "30 days."

A California girl through and through, Mique loves the beach, flip-flops, a good bean-and-cheese burrito, baseball, antiquing and getting lost in a great book.

Her biggest joy has always been cheering on her three kids—Jonathan, Julia and Andrew. She has her husband, Josh, to thank for a life of laughter, adventure and fun. They live in the Los Angeles area in California.

INDEX

TEAR-OUT DESIGNS

Dear Service Member,

You mean the WORLD to us!

Thank you for your service.

_____

_____

_____

_____

_____

_____

Glitter
SPARKLE
SHINE
BUT MOST OF ALL
BE KIND

Glitter
SPARKLE
SHINE
BUT MOST OF ALL
BE KIND

Glitter
SPARKLE
SHINE
BUT MOST OF ALL
BE KIND

Glitter
SPARKLE
SHINE
BUT MOST OF ALL
BE KIND

BLOOM
where you're planted

BLOOM
where you're planted

BLOOM
where you're planted

BLOOM
where you're planted

BLOOM
where you're planted

BLOOM
where you're planted

BLOOM
where you're planted

BLOOM
where you're planted

THANK you!

We appreciate all that
you do to protect
us and keep us safe.

THANK you!

We appreciate all that
you do to protect
us and keep us safe.

THANK you!

We appreciate all that
you do to protect
us and keep us safe.

THANK you!

We appreciate all that
you do to protect
us and keep us safe.

Let's do this!
RANDOM ACT OF
KINDNESS

Let's do this!
RANDOM ACT OF
KINDNESS

Let's do this!
RANDOM ACT OF
KINDNESS

Let's do this!
RANDOM ACT OF
KINDNESS

Family
SERVICE SCAVENGER HUNT

We are involved in a family scavenger hunt to help spread kindness throughout our neighborhood with service. Can we be of service to you? Help us check off our list.

☐ Vacuum a room
☐ Wash the dishes
☐ Take the trash out
☐ Clean up the kid toys
☐ Water the plants
☐ Feed the family pet
☐ Deliver treats

☐ Help with the laundry
☐ Clean the yard
☐ Pick up the mail
☐ Sweep the floor
☐ Wash the windows
☐ Help organize
☐ Neighbor's choice

I love you because

_____
_____
_____
_____

I appreciate you because

_____
_____
_____
_____

I care about you because

_____
_____
_____
_____

I admire you because

_____
_____
_____
_____

BE HAPPY
& SMILE

COLOR
your
out!  *heart*

No beauty shines brighter
than a kind heart.

You are the recipient of a random act of kindness.

COLOR
your
out! *heart*

No beauty shines brighter
than a kind heart.

You are the recipient of a random act of kindness.

COLOR
your
out!  *heart*

No beauty shines brighter
than a kind heart.

You are the recipient of a random act of kindness.

COLOR
your
out!  *heart*

No beauty shines brighter
than a kind heart.

You are the recipient of a random act of kindness.

Dear _____,

You are my
FAVORITE!

Thank you for everything!

_____

_____

_____

_____

_____

And when it *rains* on your parade,
look up rather than down.
Without the rain,
there would be no *rainbow*!

THINKING OF YOU! ♥ ENJOY THIS RAINBOW BOX.

And when it *rains* on your parade,
look up rather than down.
Without the rain,
there would be no *rainbow*!

THINKING OF YOU! ♥ ENJOY THIS RAINBOW BOX.

Thinking of you!

FROM OUR HOME TO YOURS

Recipe for:
Directions:

From:

Thinking of you!

FROM OUR HOME TO YOURS

Recipe for:
Directions:

From:

JUST BECAUSE

- - - - - - - - - - - - - - - - - - - -

Thinking of you today
and wanted you to know!

Please pass this plate on
to someone that you love.
We can spread some kindness
simply *just because.*

DATE NIGHT RAOK IDEA

DATE NIGHT RAOK IDEA

DATE NIGHT RAOK IDEA

DATE NIGHT RAOK IDEA

Enjoy this
RANDOM ACT OF
KINDNESS

Pay it forward when you can.
● ● ● ● ● ● ● ●

Enjoy this
RANDOM ACT OF
KINDNESS

Pay it forward when you can.
● ● ● ● ● ● ● ●

Enjoy this
RANDOM ACT OF
KINDNESS

Pay it forward when you can.
● ● ● ● ● ● ● ●

Enjoy this
RANDOM ACT OF
KINDNESS

Pay it forward when you can.
● ● ● ● ● ● ● ●

Thinking of You!

Caregiving often calls us to lean into love we didn't know possible.

-Tia Walker

Thinking of You!

Caregiving often calls us to lean into love we didn't know possible.

-Tia Walker

Thinking of You!

Caregiving often calls us to lean into love we didn't know possible.

-Tia Walker

thank you for EVERYTHING

thank you for EVERYTHING

MAKE THESE SHAPES:

MAKE THESE LETTERS & NUMBERS:

A B C D E F G H I J K L M
N O P Q R S T U V W X Y Z
1 2 3 4 5 6 7 8 9 10

SENDING YOU
HUGS &
KISSES

SENDING YOU
HUGS &
KISSES

SENDING YOU
HUGS &
KISSES

SENDING YOU
HUGS &
KISSES

THE MORE
THAT YOU
READ, THE
MORE THINGS
YOU
WILL KNOW.
THE MORE
THAT YOU
LEARN,
THE MORE
PLACES
YOU'LL GO.
-DR. SEUSS

A BOOK.
IS A
dream
THAT
YOU
HOLD
IN YOUR
HAND.

-NEIL GAIMAN

TODAY
A
READER.
TOMORROW
A
LEADER.

-MARGARET FULLER

DING DONG DONUTS

DONUT YOU KNOW HOW AWESOME YOU ARE?

DING DONG DONUTS

DONUT YOU KNOW HOW AWESOME YOU ARE?

THANK YOU FOR YOUR SERVICE!

_____

_____

_____

_____

_____

_____

THANK YOU FOR YOUR SERVICE!

_____

_____

_____

_____

_____

_____

THANK YOU FOR YOUR SERVICE!

_____

_____

_____

_____

_____

_____

THANK YOU FOR YOUR SERVICE!

_____

_____

_____

_____

_____

_____

I'm celebrating my birthday with **RANDOM** ACTS OF KINDNESS

THANKS FOR *being a part* of my special day

I'm celebrating my birthday with **RANDOM** ACTS OF KINDNESS

THANKS FOR *being a part* of my special day

I'm celebrating my birthday with **RANDOM** ACTS OF KINDNESS

THANKS FOR *being a part* of my special day

You are the recipient of a **RANDOM** ACT OF KINDNESS in honor of my birthday.
Thanks for helping me celebrate!

Free Library!

TAKE A BOOK
LEAVE A BOOK

A BOOK IS A DREAM THAT YOU HOLD IN YOUR HAND

HELLO
sunshine!

I'M
PROUD
of YOU

BE
AWESOME
TODAY

YOU
ARE
LOVED

IT DOES NOT MATTER HOW SLOWLY YOU GO AS LONG AS YOU DO NOT STOP.

-CONFUCIUS

KEEP YOUR EYES ON THE STARS, AND YOUR FEET ON THE GROUND.

-THEODORE ROOSEVELT

BE KIND WHENEVER POSSIBLE. IT IS ALWAYS POSSIBLE.
-DALAI LAMA

AIM FOR THE MOON. IF YOU MISS, YOU MAY HIT A STAR.
-W. CLEMENT STONE

first aid kit

first aid kit

first aid kit

SHARE THE BOUNTY

We all share the same garden. When you water another's you water your own.

TAKE SOME NOW.
LEAVE SOME LATER.